## Foreword

I dedicate this b
who is a Pastor and my Mother who passed away
8 years ago. They were my inspiration they intro-
duced me to God as a toddler and then set a life example for me to follow centered around faith in God.
I can honestly say I do not know where I would be
today without having the strong spiritual training, I
received from both my parents growing up and it has
continued to be the foundation of our family today.
I love you both and I am forever thankful for all you
taught me I remember just about everything includ-
ing the stern but much needed discipline and even
the awfully long days in church.

## Spiritual Perspective

Good things come from having a disciplined lifestyle great thing come when you add wisdom and knowledge to your disciplined lifestyle. If you want to accomplish anything in life it all starts with self-discipline, especially in your spiritual life. If you observe your surroundings every day, you will notice changes first subtle then more definitive. As you begin understanding the seasons in your life you will see subtle changes at first and then very definitive changes in your life, Understanding seasons is a treasure that's been lying in the darkness in most of our lives. If you find yourself looking for answers to questions that arise in the normal course of your life. Then you need a better understanding of the seasons in your life remember seasons are a spiritual law they are unaffected by anything we can experience. So, In the time of a pandemic and uncertainty in the economy you have to lean on spiritual laws they are not affected by natural laws. I have found when I take a spiritual perspective to finding the solution, I usually find it  But like all matters with God its going to require discipline from you if your serious about getting the answer to your question or issue, you're going to have to be disciplined because the solution is going to require you to do something you are not accustomed to and it will probably be uncomfortable for you to do. So, you are going to have to be disciplined enough to do what is required even though it doesn't feel comfortable for you. But the end result will be worth the sacrifice. It is also important to remember the discipline you exercised to get your desired result must be sustained to prevent the same or a similar problem from occurring again. It is the same with Seasons once you apply the discipline you need to understand the seasons in your life you will create a lifestyle that's easily managed and one that you can sustain for the remainder of your life, Seasons are a Spirtual law that will allow you to reap great results in your life and business. It requires discipline but the benefits can be immeasurable to you. This book series " The Seasons in your life" will enlighten your eyes to the benefits of living your life following the principles of the spiritual laws that have been put in place to ensure our having a more abundant life free from regrets.. This book the first in the series will help you to find your Purpose by helping you to gain an understanding that your purpose has seasons, and knowing which season your in can help you  navigate through your life in peaceful order and see with clarity.

## Predestined

Many believe that all of us are the result of a Predestined life. I also believe that, and I believe that our life can go many different directions based on the decisions we make during our life. I also believe that a lot of people have not discovered their purpose as of yet and they are living their life with a veil of uncertainty about their purpose on this earth. Now with that being said I also believe that we are all called to something and whatever decisions you have made in your life and whatever journey you have taken and whatever obstacles you have encountered, I believe you are exactly where you are supposed to be, reading what you are supposed to be reading and feeling what you are supposed to be feeling. When it is time for you to start your calling, it will happen for some sooner and others later. When it is time it will happen. What do I do now you may wonder? I say to you from this time right now and going forward start preparing yourself to be the best you can be, start by strengthening areas in your life you consider weaknesses. Look in the mirror and be honest with yourself and attack your weaknesses, I am here to tell you that the time may be near for you or it may not be. But what will happen is that you will be able to understand the process and this will ease your mind and allow you to prepare in peace with a clear mind.

## God's Order

"Everything has a season, and a time to every Purpose under the heaven. A time to be born and a time to die, a time to plant and a time to harvest what has been planted."

I have never heard a compelling argument that

can dispute everything has a season and I know I never will. You see my life really changed when I acknowledged that I was not in control and there was someone greater calling the shots and I didn't have the ability to stop spiritual laws that were put in effect no matter what I tried. I'm not talking about acknowledgement with words I'm talking about acknowledgement with actions that consisted of changing my ways and my way of doing things. Which meant my heart had to change, at that point I began seeing life from a bigger picture not just seeing in my bubble everything that encompassed my life and family circle but seeing the bigger picture of what affects my city, state, country and community. When you get outside of yourself and start looking at city, state, national and world issues, and problems you have now entered into the realm of "God's Order". These issues and problems are too big for any one individual to solve by his or her own means so you have to access something greater and that can only be done with "God's Order" let me tell you there's such a power exchange that takes place when you submit to the fact that God is all Power. Let's talk in more detail about this you see the world was created to maintain and sustain its occupants. everything we need is here all we ever needed was the knowledge, which I like to refer to as earths operating manual. and it has been laid out in a manner in which the previous advances of the generations before us we have been able to take their advancements and use them to create our advancements just as the generations before us did and as will the generations that follow us   Okay let me reel this back into the subject of this book "Understanding the Sea-

sons in Your Life" This is the most powerful knowledge for you to have and it will change your life if
you exercise the discipline to obtain the knowledge,
and apply it in your life you will see great results in
your life. It works the same way as your knowledge
of the seasons of the year, when it is winter you were
a coat, hat and scarf. In the summer you break out
the shorts because its hot weather and a jacket in the
spring and fall. these are spiritual laws they never
change. and it is the same with the seasons in your
life once you identify what season you are in then
you can prepare accordingly.

**Manifestation?**

The question everyone wants the answer to. When
will I see the manifestation? I am going to use the
story of Jesus as my example I hope you do not mind
He is someone that most everyone has heard of. He
was said to have lived 33 years on this earth with the
first 30 years in relative quiet obscurity. But from
ages 30-33 or let us say the last 3 years of his life He
was fulfilling his purpose doing His work with miracles of all kinds. The instant miracle manifestations were normal for Him, Why not us? Let us look
a little closer at the first 30 years of His life. He lived
like us no manifestations no instant miracles. So, I
concluded that His ages 0-30 it was not time, or He
had not entered His season of manifestation in His
purpose, but from age 30-33. It was time He did His
first miracle helping a bridegroom who ran out of
wine at his wedding, although Jesus appeared to be
unaware until Mary asked Him, but once asked, He
did the first of what would be many miracles to follow. So, what do we gleam from this? when it is time
manifestation will happen. What do we do while we

wait? We prepare ourselves. Jesus prepared the first 30 years of His life but when it was time it happened. . I put together a guide that has been helpful for me in understanding where I am in my season. It is important to understand that your purpose has seasons. They evolve and adapt to you and your circumstances. Knowing what season, you are in will greatly benefit you and help you manage your own expectations as well as others. It is important to get this information branded in your heart. A farmer knows based on when he plants seed when he will reap the harvest. There are stages he goes thru from the time he plants until the time he reaps, but he knows what to expect every season unless something beyond his control occurs. It is the same with each of us, knowing the season and understanding them will allow you to be at peace while operating with the same power and authority as Jesus did in His purpose. Jesus ages 30-33 was never out of season while those around Him marveled at His works but all He was doing was fulfilling His purpose. It will be the same for you when you are in your season of manifestation. The key for you is understanding the Seasons in your purpose, they never change they just evolve and adapt to your circumstances, So, you always want to be in season. Jesus started at age 30 Moses started at age 80 so age should be of no concern to you. When you understand the seasons in your purpose then you will have the life you desire. The question I here so often is, when will it happen? The answer is directly linked to what Season you are in. So, just as a farmer knows when to plant his seed he also knows when he can reap his harvest. The seasons never change year after year, but the farmer will evolve by improving what he is doing to increase his harvest and decrease the possibility of problems arising with his harvest. Can I speed up the Process? When it is time the manifestation will happen. This should remove the pressure of you trying to figure out when will it happen. Does a farmer know how to make his harvest come sooner? No, he can't change the seasons, but he can be better prepared each season that comes around based on his previous year's experiences. What am I saying? Based on his past experiences he cannot change the seasons, but he can multiply and increase the size of his harvest by what he has learned during the process. by multiplying what works and subtracting what does not work.

## Purpose has four Seasons:

1). Calling

2). Preparation

3). Manifestation

4). Rest

## Seasons in Your Purpose

1). Calling. *This stage you are receiving "understanding and revelation" of what your purpose is.

2). Preparation. *This stage you're getting the "wisdom and knowledge" you need for your purpose

3). Manifestation. *This stage "action and doing" you have the Authority and wisdom to begin your purpose

4). Rest. *This stage "meditation and evaluation" on what you're doing and have done so you can make adjustments or changes to improve.

## How do I know?

All your experiences along the way should help you. It's really simple if you don't know your purpose then you are in the first season "Calling" and you stay there until you know what your purpose is. How can you go to the next season which is "Preparation" until you know what to prepare for. If you know what your calling is and have not started, then you know your still in preparation. keep the discipline to not rush the process but learn to trust the process.

## How do I know my Purpose?

This is a simple question with a simple answer. Your Purpose is what you gravitate to and the closer you come to the time for you to begin it will become clearer for you to see and can appear like its drawing you towards it. One thing I can assure you when it is time you will know it. Now it's important for you to not stress out because you don't know your purpose its ok it's not time yet remember the closer you get the clearer it will become for you. Remember Jesus started at 30 after being in the temples at age 12 knowing who He himself was but it took another 18 years before He started. Moses did not start until the age of 80 and had to travel thru a desert at the age of 80 to begin. So, these two examples make it clear that age is not the determining factor when it comes to fulfilling your purpose. Here's a couple nuggets for you regarding your purpose it is easy for you to do probably something you have done before and when you do it you get a satisfaction deep inside of you. Your life's journey is working hand in hand with your purpose, all the experiences you've gained is playing a role in preparing you for your purpose so you never have to worry everything is doing its part for you. As you discover your Purpose and get more familiar with each season you will find such a comfort moving forward understanding that where you are today is exactly where you are supposed to be. 20 years ago, I was in prayer asking God for a laundry list of what I wanted and He said to me you need to understand the seasons in your life and be wise in your understanding of this. I didn't think much about it because it wasn't on the ridiculous list of things I was asking Him for, But fast forward 20 years to now and I realize He was giving me the answer to how to get the realistic things on my list then, Ok don't act like I'm the only one to ask God for unrealistic things, anyway good people I now realize He gave me the answer 20 years ago with one simple statement "you need to understand the seasons in your life".

Wow how could this simple statement be the key to all that I was asking for? And why did I need to be wise in my understanding this? It is as simple as this, everything we do in life revolves around a season it has taken me over 20 years and a lot of heartache, pain and tears to understand this. When God answers us, His answers are complete and all-knowing, and you don't have to ask Him to do it again because His answers come finished. Let me explain it this way. If there is a golden egg and a baby goose that will eventually over time grow up to lay golden eggs which would you take? The majority of people are conditioned to take the egg because of their needs they feel have to be met now,. But they definitely have a lack of understanding in this matter The egg is our fix it's what we have received since we were a child if we want something we ask our parents or another adult for it and we get it unless it could bring us harm or it's something we don't need. Our parents when we are a child do not tell us to go get a job so you can buy your own school clothes or ice cream cone etc. That is not parenting from a spiritual perspective that's parenting from a basis of love to meet a immediate need. God is love so He doesn't have to parent us from a basis of love only He parent's us so that we can be complete in our life and be in a position to constantly create, manage and sustain our life and our purpose. God would give us the baby goose that lays the golden eggs because the golden eggs the baby goose produces when it grows up will meet all of our financial needs and we would not have to go back to God to ask for that need again, because the baby goose He gave us was a complete and finished answer to our need. If you think about some accounts in the bible were, He gave one man 10 talents another 5 and another 1 He always rewarded the person for taking what they had and expanding or increasing it. I think you would agree with me that the man that was given the 10 talents would take the baby goose over the golden egg. That is clearly operating from a spiritual perspective and by doing that the spiritual results come into play and that is getting complete answers to problems and issues. not temporary fixes that usually end up costing you more and creating additional issues in the long run. But the problem is that we can be so moment driven that we can't see the complete answer or we see the complete answer but we have no self-discipline to do what we need to do to recieve the complete answer. In the example having self-discipline would be taking the baby goose and taking care of it until it started laying the golden eggs that would be used to meet the financial needs for years to come. If you ask God, He's going to give you an answer from a spiritual perspective that is going to be complete and finished, remember He sees the end from the beginning. So, His answers will be your end. I ask you to remember that God's answers to us are our end as you continue to read through this book. There have been many experiments done where an animal will have an invisible barrier placed over it and every time the animal tries to get out because the barrier is invisible its hits it and falls back down again and again until eventually the barrier is removed and the animal by all accounts is free but it doesn't even try because it thinks the barrier is still there. I didn't intend to go here but God intended for me to go here so that everyone who is reading this book is getting the revealed knowledge from God that the barriers are removed from your life and all that you have dreamed and stopped pursuing its time to pursue again because it is the season for your dreams to manifest. If you can get yourself to start moving on it, God will see it thru remember when you got the dream or idea from God He saw the end when you were looking at the beginning, He saw the results when you were looking at the task. "Hallelujah, Thank you Lord" somebody reading this right now understands you put your all into that dream and your blood sweat and tears and you began to think to no avail, but I got news for you  "YOU ARE NOT FINISHED YOU ARE JUST BEGINNING" I don't usually quote a lot of scriptures when I write because I don't want to lose anybody I know when I get a word from God for the person that hears it they are in a unique frame of mind where the word will settle in their heart so they can think about it time and time again.  But I just sense that some people are tired and don't know if they can get the strength back to go after their dream or promise from God. So for you I'll quote this scripture it is found in Isaiah 55th chapter starting at verse 10 and since we have International readers I'm quoting from the New International version of the bible you can use whatever version you choose it all means the same, I quote: verse 10: As the rain and snow come down from heaven and do not return to it without watering the earth and making it bud and flourish so that it yields seed for the sower and bread for the eater. verse 11: So is my word that goeth forth out of my mouth; It will not return to me empty but will accomplish what I desire and achieve the purpose for which I sent it. verse 12" You will go out in joy and be led forth in peace the mountains and the hills will burst into song before you and all the trees of the field will clap their hands. verse 13: Instead of the thornbush will grow the juniper, and instead of briers the myrtle will grow This will be for the Lord's renown for an everlasting sign that will endure forever"!!!!!!! Glory to the most High I say again Glory to the most High!!!!! So you may say I tried everything and it didn't work, you just don't understand. I may say its ok you were just out of Season; you were not in your Season of manifestation so no matter what you would have tried it would not have worked then. But this is your Season of manifestation and it will work now. It's no different than it was for Jesus in ages 0-30 no miracles, no manifestation and just like His mother Mary had to tell Him to help the bridegroom with the wine, God is using this book to tell you it's time All the Barriers are removed from your life just like the animal test I discussed earlier were the animals stayed put because they didn't know they were free. I'm telling you now you're free to go and you will have the desired end. But before you take-off let's talk about a couple things that are really important. First you have to remember that if this is your season of manifestation then as you move forward do so responsibly so that when this season ends you can be like Joseph and be prepared for a drought because he saved, stored up and had a plan. That plan has to come from God so that means you have to spend some time in prayer with Him and you should probably review your plan and update it because you know now what didn't work for you in the past and identify that season you were in so you will be prepared the next time that season comes around. Remember we talked about the farmer not being able to change the seasons, but he can make adjustments that will allow him to increase his harvest in harvest season by what he learned in his past experiences. I'm going to throw in some principles that you should incorporate into your lifestyle. God will not give you more than you can manage nor should you ever want more than you can manage., So that means you're going to have to use self-discipline and become a great manager.

You are going to have to understand the Seasons in your life and business by doing this you will be prepared for whatever comes your way and by understanding spiritual laws you will always be in front of whatever comes your direction. Learn to create, learn to be able to manage what you create, then always be able to sustain what you create, or don't create it all, for it will fail. As we look around today where are living in unprecedented times uncertainty everywhere and in the midst of a Pandemic. It would be easy to say I'm going to wait it out and see what happens. History is full of people who have done that for its not the first time the world has faced a crisis and recovered. Then you find the person that looks around and sees many opportunities much as Caleb did when he went to Joshua and said I'm getting old I want to see the promise from God, you don't have to go with me, but many years ago I saw the promise land and we didn't go then

So I ask you now before I'm to old can I go, and that prompted the move of the Children of Israel into the promise land. God using one man to move His nation. I'm sure you have probably heard before the phrase the only thing that can stop you is yourself. I can think of many accounts where people in the bible would press on and by pressing on, they were successful. The point I'm making is for the chosen few these days are the days of opportunities and fulfilled promises so go get yours, I believe the next 7 years are years of immense opportunity for those who have been positioned well, and can see and understand this season we are in today. I would like to challenge you to move on beyond what you can see in front of you and close your natural eyes and open your spiritual eyes and see what God is doing and what He has for you. Write down what He has told you if you have already written them down then pull them out again and review them because everything has a season even your understanding of a plan of God. I will give you one of my examples every year I fast and pray for 7 days prior to the new year coming so I can see what's coming in the new year for me my family and the world. So at end of December 2019 I fasted and prayed and took notes of what God was saying to me. I remember how different this fast was for me it was hard and then on the last day I felt like I needed to rest. I remember writing I feel what God must have felt after He created the earth on the 7th day. Of course, I can't imagine what He must have felt but I just felt something different than what I was accustomed to. I looked up and before I knew it The world has shut down and panic is setting into this nation, and it keeps going and going and I go back to my notes from the fast and I don't see anything about a pandemic so to keep it real with you. I got mad at God here we go again so I'm the only person that gets mad at God. Ok just pray for me, anyway good people I was really furious how could after 7 days of fasting and praying God does not tell me this. My faith took a real hit I started questioning everything God had told me, of course I did how could He tell me about my future wife when

He would not tell me about a Pandemic.... Thankfully for me again, God ignored me and did not strike me down. But instead after me putting Him on punishment for a couple months I decided to give Him a chance to redeem Himself to me and bail me out of this mess I was in with my business shutting down and no end in sight, it was the least He could do right? Well I may have exaggerated a little and left out the part where I was on my face crying and begging Him to rescue me and not let me be wiped out. But hey it is just a small detail I forgot to mention. And yes, we know God comes to my rescue by telling me to get my notes out from the fast and lets go thru them. So, I did and what I found was God had told me what was about to happen but because I had not seen or experienced anything like this I didn't understand it. what He was showing to me was when it was time for me to get it I would. Let us just say my season for understanding was enlightened so that I could see it. I had the audacity to challenge God's integrity unknowingly to me because I was mad at Him, but His grace kept me. Then after reading and going through my notes again with my understanding enlightened, I came to the realization that we are in the greatest time to grow, increase, overtake and conquer all. I believe that in this season if your fortunate enough for God to have revealed to you that all the barriers are removed that has held us back and all we have to do is keep pressing toward the mark. I found out that God takes it personal when He is challenged and I say to you that every promise He has made to you during this season if you will do your part because He has already done His you will see the power of God manifest in your life like never before, Remember He has spoken the end from the beginning to you, and I think you have some ends that are going to come to pass for you now. I would encourage you to discipline yourself to understand the seasons in your purpose so you begin to see the life you desire every time you look in the mirror and no matter what's going on around you just no God is with you now and forever.

## Epilogue

The subjects of purpose and season has been of great importance to me for over 20 years I've searched just like you have looking for clarity on how to know it and understand it and most importantly when will it happen. The results of my research and meditation led me to write this book in hopes that it would help you discover the importance of understanding the seasons of your purpose and life. It was intentionally kept short and simple so it would be easy for you to grasp and understand. I hope that after reading this you can better understand the season you're in and reap the benefits in your life. I would also recommend that you read this book over and over because you will see different things every time you read it. I have put blank pages at the end of this book so you can write your notes and refer to them like a study guide.

# NOTES:

_____
_____
_____
_____
_____
_____
_____
_____
_____
_____
_____
_____
_____
_____
_____
_____
_____
_____
_____
_____
_____
_____
_____
_____
_____

---

K.C. STEVENSON

Made in the USA
Columbia, SC
30 August 2020